Worm

Jill Bailey

Heinemann
LIBRARY

www.heinemann.co.uk/library
Visit our website to find out more information about Heinemann Library books.

To order:

 Phone 44 (0) 1865 888066

 Send a fax to 44 (0) 1865 314091

 Visit the Heinemann Bookshop at www.heinemann.co.uk/library to browse our catalogue and order online.

First published in Great Britain by Heinemann Library, Halley Court, Jordan Hill, Oxford OX2 8EJ, part of Harcourt Education.
Heinemann is a registered trademark of Harcourt Education Ltd.

Editorial: Clare Lewis and Katie Shepherd
Design: Ron Kamen, Michelle Lisseter and Bridge Creative Services Limited
Illustrations: Alan Fraser at Pennant Illustration
Picture Research: Maria Joannou
Production: Helen McCreath

Printed and bound in China by South China Printers

13 digit ISBN 978 0 431 01837 9 (hardback)
10 09 08 07 06
10 9 8 7 6 5 4 3 2 1

13 digit ISBN 978 0 431 01901 7 (paperback)
11 10 09 08 07
10 9 8 7 6 5 4 3 2 1

British Library Cataloguing in Publication Data
Bailey, Jill
Bug Books: Worm - 2nd Edition
592.3
A full catalogue record for this book is available from the British Library.

Acknowledgements
The publishers would like to thank the following for permission to reproduce photographs:
Alamy Images p.**8** (Graphic Science); Ardea London Ltd pp.**6** (JP Ferrero), **4** (P Morris); Bruce Coleman Ltd pp. **5** (Dr F Sauer), **18** (K Taylor); FLPA pp.**16, 22** (G Hyde), **24** (M Rose), **27** (M Thomas), **20, 21** (Konrad Wothe/Minden Pictures); Getty Images/Photodisc p.**26**; Chris Honeywell p.**28**; NHPA p.**11** (D Woodfall); Oxford Scientific Film: pp.**17, 29** (K Atkinson), **23** (J Cooke), **9** (B Davidson), **25** (C Milkins), **19** (R Redfern), **15** (H Taylor), **6, 7, 12, 13, 14** (D Thompson).

Cover photograph reproduced with permission of Photolibrary.com/Oxford Scientific Films.

The publishers would like to thank Nancy Harris for her assistance in the preparation of this book.

Every effort has been made to contact copyright holders of any material reproduced in this book. Any omissions will be rectified in subsequent printings if notice is given to the publishers.

Any words appearing in the text in bold, **like this**, are explained in the Glossary

Contents

What are worms?

head

tail

Worms are long, thin, and soft. They do not have legs. A worm's head is rounded and its tail is more pointed.

The **saddle** round the worm's middle makes a slippery slime called mucus. This helps the worm to slip easily through soil. There are lots of different types of worm. We are going to look at earthworms.

saddle

An earthworm has no eyes or ears.
Its whole body can taste and feel.
You can see a long, thin tube inside
the worm. This carries blood all
along the worm.

An earthworm's body is made up of lots of parts. Each part has a few small, stiff hairs called **bristles**. They act like tiny hooks. They help the worm move along.

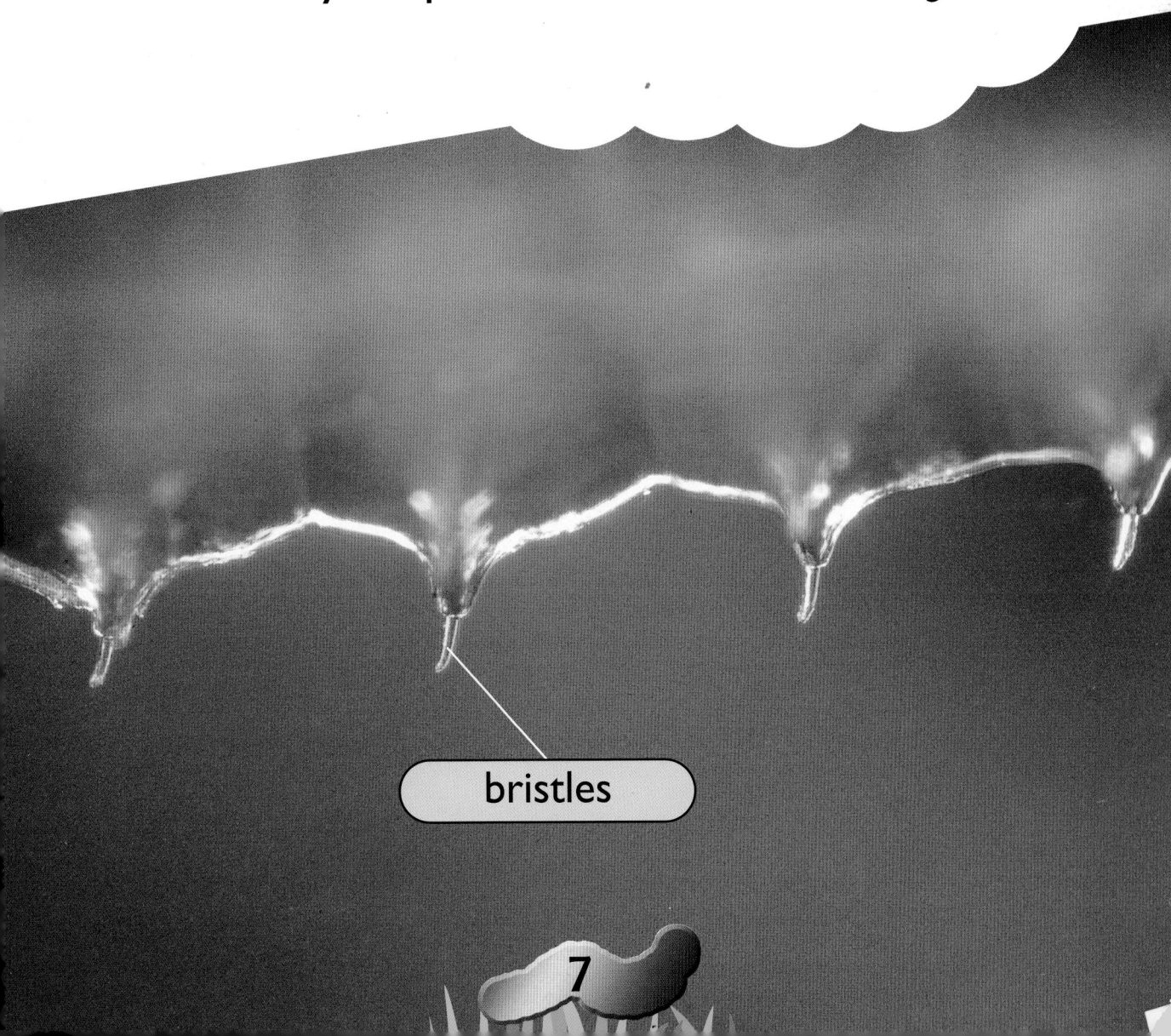

bristles

The smallest kind of worm is only as long as your little fingernail. A small earthworm is about the same size as your finger. A long earthworm could stretch from your fingertips to your elbow.

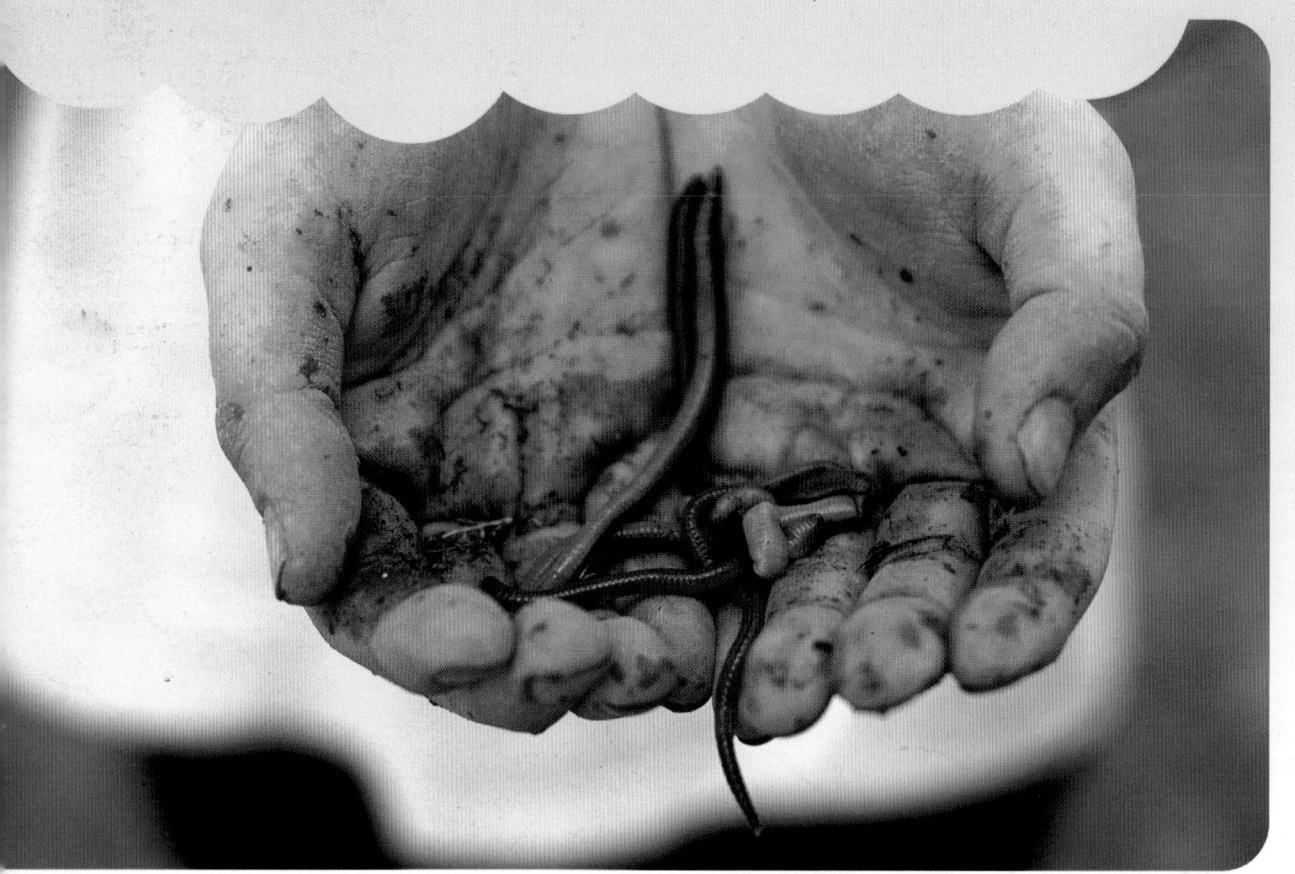

The biggest earthworms in the world can be the length of four grown-ups lying end to end. They can be as wide as two fingers side by side.

Where do worms live?

Worms live in holes called **burrows** in the soil. Usually they live near the surface. In very dry or cold weather they may tunnel down much deeper.

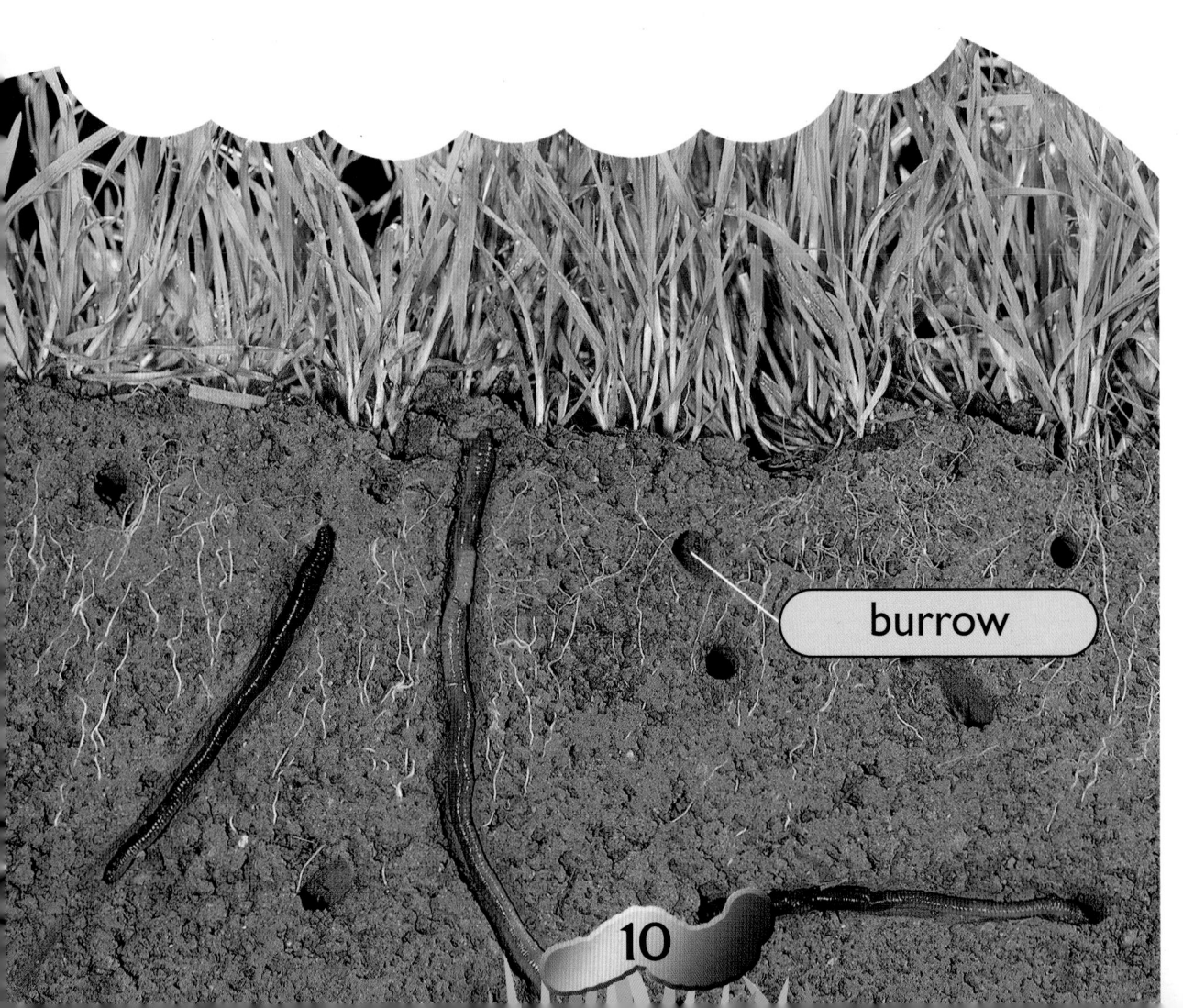

burrow

Worms live anywhere where there is soil. In old grassland like this, you could find lots of worms.

How are worms born?

On warm, damp summer evenings, worms come out of their **burrows** to **mate**. The female worm lays eggs.

Each worm makes a thick slime.
The slime goes hard to make a
case called a **cocoon** for the eggs.

cocoon

A worm may lay up to 20 eggs inside each **cocoon**, but usually only one survives. The cocoon keeps it safe until it is ready to **hatch**.

After one to five months the baby hatches from the cocoon. It is very tiny and stays hidden in the soil. It will take at least a year to grow as big as its parents.

What do worms eat?

Worms eat the parts of dead plants and animals that they find in the soil. They also eat the soil as they tunnel.

They break down the soil to get the food inside it. The useless grains of soil pass out of the worm's tail end. Sometimes the waste soil makes small heaps.

waste soil

Which animals eat worms?

Many birds, mice, hedgehogs, and other animals eat worms. They listen for the sound of the worm moving, then they dig it up.

Worms also have enemies underground. Moles dig tunnels through the soil to look for worms. Moles cannot see in the dark, but they can hear and smell.

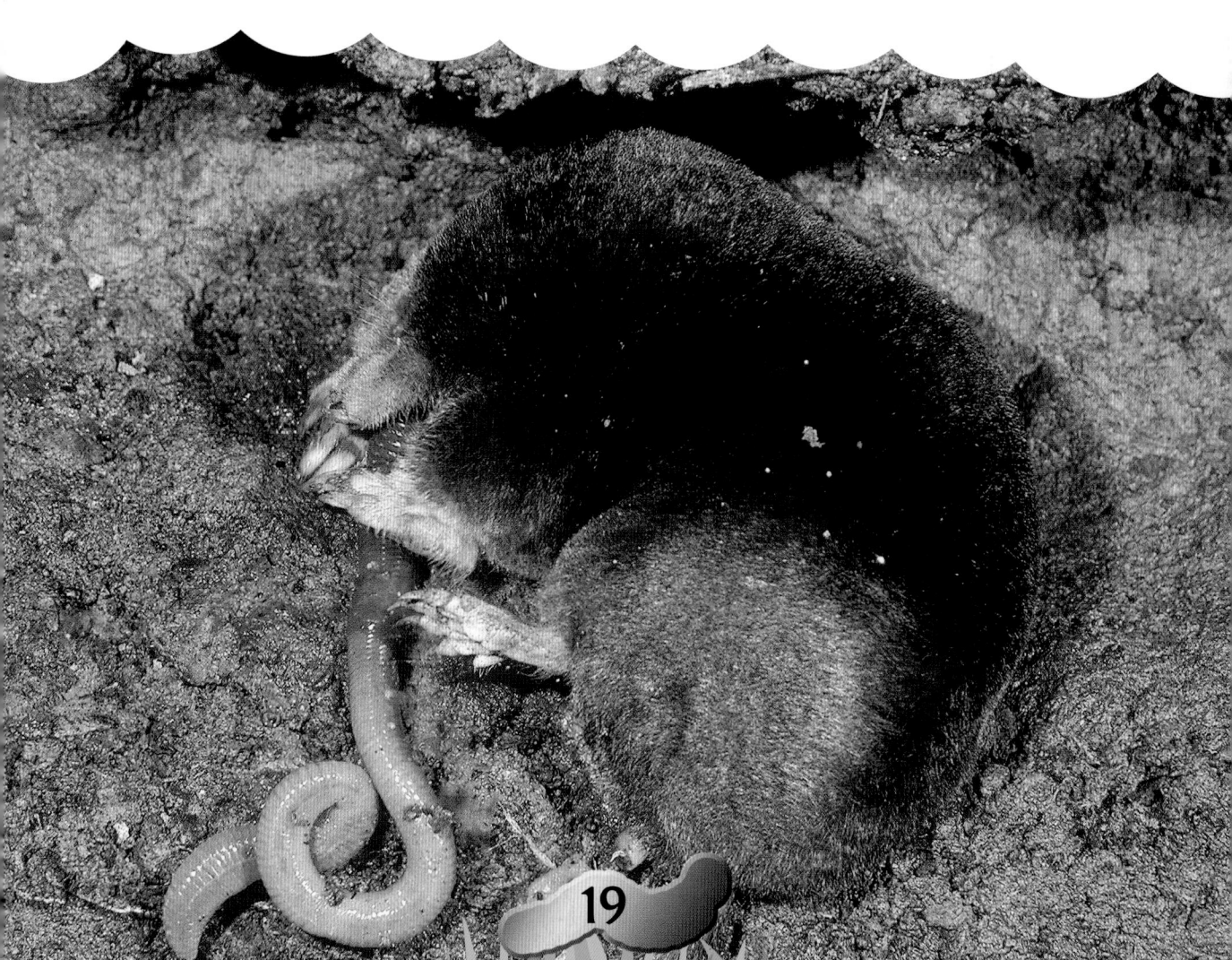

How do worms move?

A worm's soft body is filled with a watery liquid. The worm can squeeze its body into different shapes. To move forward, the worm makes its front end long and thin.

Then it digs the stiff hairs called **bristles** into the ground and pulls its tail end forward. Now it digs in the bristles on its tail and lets go of the front ones as it stretches forward again.

How long do worms live?

A baby worm takes about a year to grow big enough to have its own babies. It can then live for another 10 years.

Worms cling so hard to their **burrows** that if birds try to pull them out, their bodies may break in half. Sometimes one half grows back into a worm. Can you see the new part of this worm?

What do worms do?

Worms spend most of their time underground. They push their way through soil, or dig with their mouths.

On warm, damp nights, worms may come to the surface of the soil. They drag dead leaves back into their **burrows** to eat.

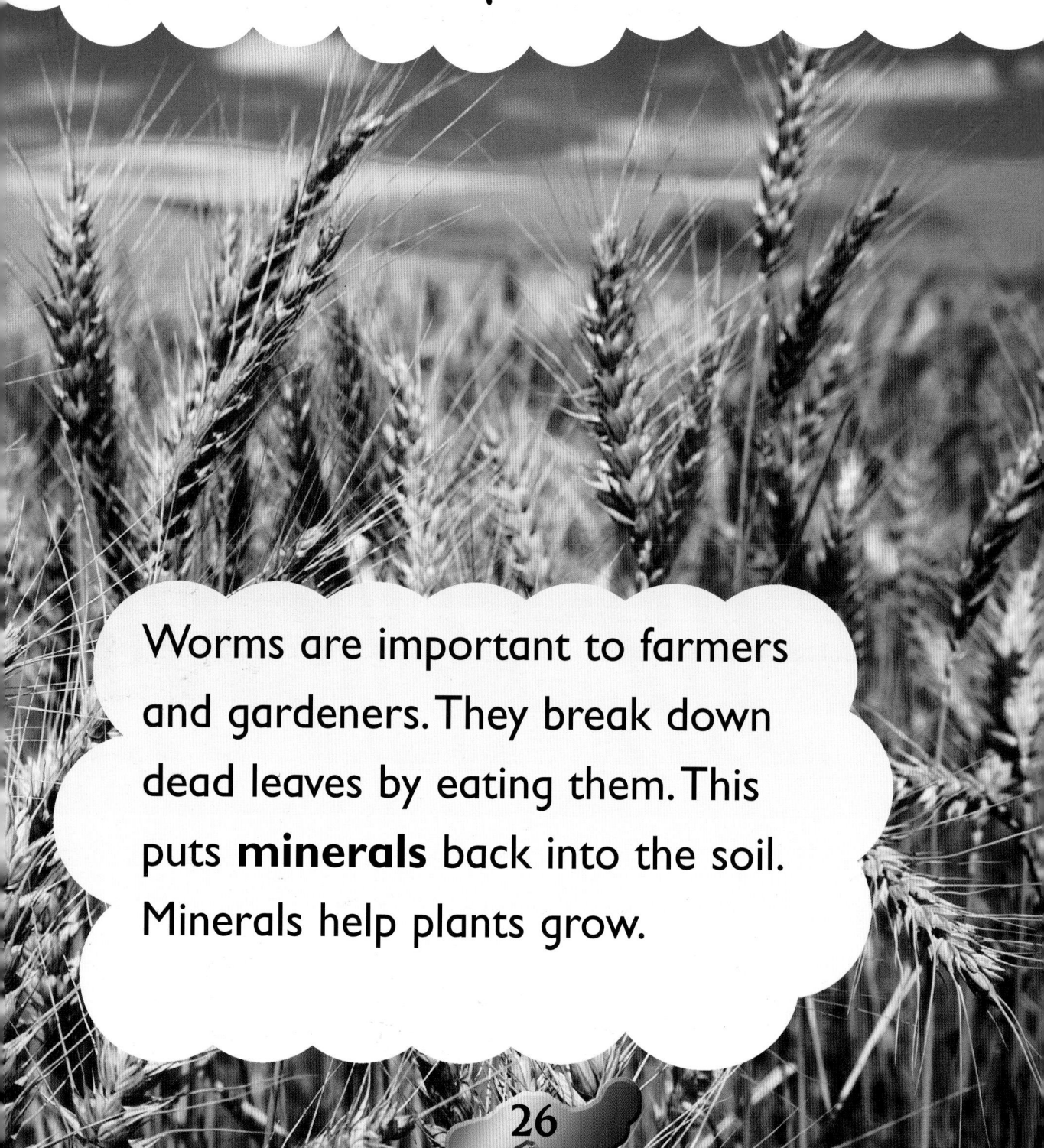

How are worms special?

Worms are important to farmers and gardeners. They break down dead leaves by eating them. This puts **minerals** back into the soil. Minerals help plants grow.

Worms move a lot of soil as they move around. Worm **burrows** let air and rain into the soil. This keeps the soil light and airy.

Thinking about worms

See for yourself how a worm changes its shape. Fill a balloon almost full of water and tie it up. Now squeeze it. It will get long and thin.

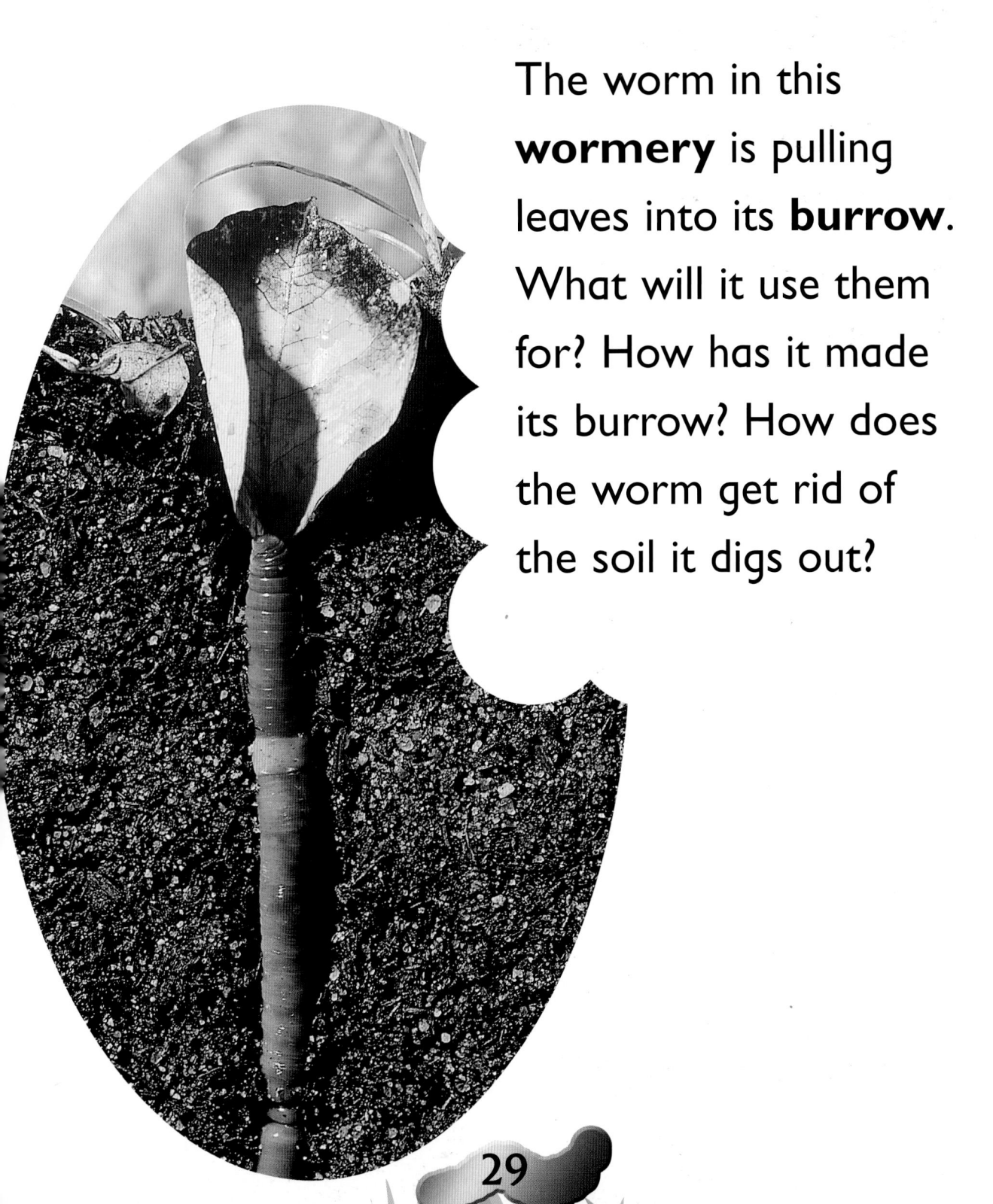

The worm in this **wormery** is pulling leaves into its **burrow**. What will it use them for? How has it made its burrow? How does the worm get rid of the soil it digs out?

Bug map

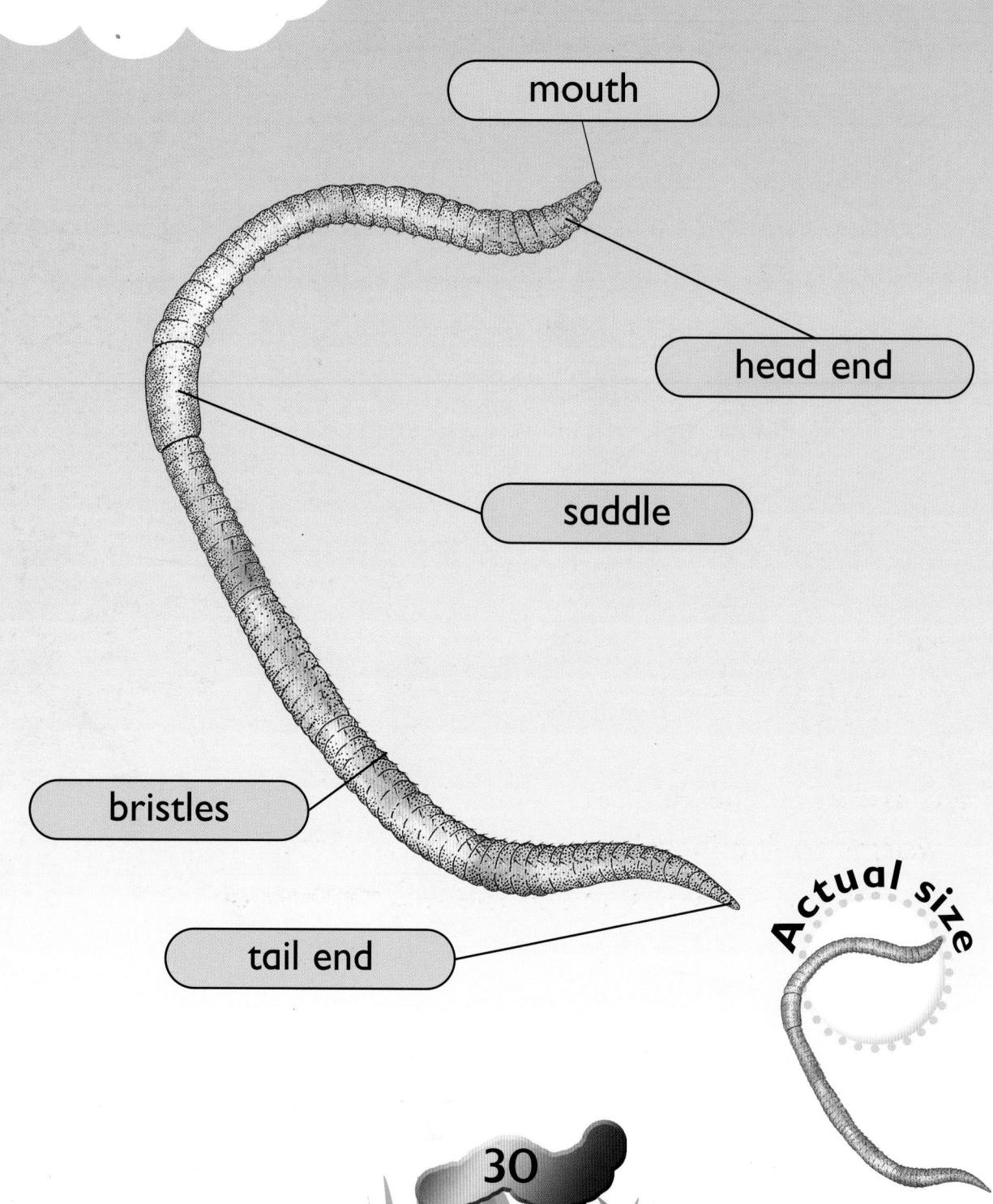

mouth

head end

saddle

bristles

tail end

Actual size

Glossary

bristles small, very stiff hairs that help the worm to grip the soil as it moves

burrow a hole that an animal makes in the ground

cocoon a tiny hard case that protects the eggs and baby worms until they hatch

hatch to come out of an egg or cocoon

mate when two creatures come together to make babies

minerals special food that animals and plants need to live

saddle a slimy band around the middle of the worm. It makes the slime that protects the worm's eggs.

wormery a special home made by people for worms to live in. It is usually made of glass and wood, and you can see the worms through the glass.

Index

More books to read

Creepy Creatures: Earthworms, Sue Barraclough (Heinemann Library, 2005)